Contents

Level Up Your Mental Game

Mental Training for Tumbling

and Overcoming Mental Blocks

Jarom Perry

Written by: Jarom Perry

Edited by: Sierra Johnson and Michelle Perry

Cover Design by: Liedke Design

1st Edition

Introduction

Tumbling requires physical and mental mastery. You can find an abundance of information on the physical techniques and conditioning required to excel. However, one of the most important aspects, mental mastery, has somehow gone relatively unaddressed in our sport. This book changes that. With the tools you will learn in this book, you can develop the mental skills required to build a healthy and positive mindset, a strong mental game and confidence like you've never known before. Utilizing this mindset will help you reach your peak performance in tumbling and anything else you set your mind to.

You may have noticed I used the word mastery in the opening sentence. When we view learning new skills through the lens of developing mastery, we tap into a powerful mental tool known as a growth mindset. In this book I will explain what the author Carol Dweck means by a 'growth mindset' in her book Mindset and how it relates to developing a strong mental game in tumbling.

Another term I use in this book, that is related to a growth mindset, is adopting a beginner's mind. A beginner's mind is one open to learning and helps you maintain the knowledge that no matter how good you get at something; you still have more you can learn. Becoming a master at something takes dedicated practice and a willingness to take on a beginner's mind at all stages of your progress.

There is an old saying that practice makes perfect, but I recently heard a better version; practice makes progress.

Trying to attain perfection is generally unattainable and sets you up for a great amount of disappointment and a negative self-image. However, everyone can master a skill and have it boost their self-esteem. As you will find out later in this book, anything that builds your self-esteem and brings in positive emotions will help you to succeed, anything that causes stress and a negative self-image will inhibit your performance.

Because of how powerful it is, our mindset is probably the most pivotal thing we can control that directly affects our performance. When we view failed attempts as a part of the process that are necessary to attain the level of mastery, our entire outlook shifts. Instead of looking at mistakes as failures, look at them as a tool for learning and improving. Staying positive through adversity keeps our body strong and your performance at its best.

Throughout this book, you will see how awareness is the basis for change. It is very hard to change something that we are not aware of. From a logical perspective, it would seem that if we can physically do something then we must be aware of it. However, this is not necessarily true. Bringing our attention to a specific body part during a skill will demonstrate this. If we are not aware of what our legs are doing in a back handspring then it will be difficult to get them straight, that is, until we've developed the muscle memory to the point it can be on autopilot without our immediate attention.

Developing good body awareness is an important skill for tumbling. It also has the added benefit of teaching us mindfulness and presence.

You might be wondering what mindfulness is. Essentially mindfulness is the act of being 100% mentally present in whatever you are doing. An example is, when you are doing a back handspring you are thinking of and focused on the back handspring and not concerned about what homework you have to do. Your mind gets into a quiet state where your focus is at its peak.

An example of not being mindful is: when you leave your house and lock the door while you're busy thinking ten different things you might forget that you just locked it. Then you end up going back to check if it's locked. Whereas if you were in a state of mindfulness when you locked the door you could easily remember that you had. Mindfulness is about being in the moment and paying direct attention to what you are doing. The really cool thing about mindfulness is that you learn faster, retain more, make fewer mistakes, and feel more fulfilled.

There is a phenomenon that you may have experienced that is directly related to mindfulness: being in a state of flow. Flow can easily be understood as: the state of being where you are so physically and mentally synced with the activity you are doing that everything else seems to disappear and the activity takes on an almost effortless quality. The external world gets quiet and your focus is so strong that it feels like you are one with the activity. There are a lot of sports that have the potential to naturally put the participant into a state of flow; tumbling is one of them, along with running, rock climbing, skiing/snowboarding, etc. Getting into the state of flow is an amazing experience and you start to crave it the more you do it. You will learn mental skills in this book to help get you into the state of flow faster.

You might be asking yourself at this point, 'why haven't my coaches taught me all this before?' Well, from a coaching perspective teaching the physical elements is way easier than the mental. For this reason, a lot of coaches struggle to help kids through the plateaus in progression or through mental blocks.

Congratulations on taking this aspect into your own hands instead of relying strictly on others to help you along. Developing a powerful base of self-esteem and self-confidence will help you excel. Following the steps in this book to take your mental training to the level of mastery will open up new doors and take your tumbling, and life, to new heights. Heights you may not even expect or imagine at this point.

If you are a coach reading this then huge props to you for developing new skills that will set you apart from the rest of the coaching world.

How to use this book most effectively:

I feel like sometimes people aren't quite sure the best way to approach a book like this. Should you jump around from page to page, chapter to chapter? Or is it best to start at the beginning and go straight through? Should you read it fast or take breaks to absorb the material and practice?

I recommend reading it in order because a lot of principles build upon each other. Take your time to absorb the material by thinking about how it pertains to your life and how you can integrate it in specific situations. Just like learning a back handspring, learning the mental tricks in this book takes practice and thoughtful consideration of what you are doing. Expect to make mistakes, to have it feel hard or feel like it might not be working as fast as you'd like. But know, that if you stick with it, as you have done with learning the physical skills, your mental game will improve and take your entire tumbling to new heights.

On that note, I also understand that a lot of people will see a section and jump straight to it because it feels most relevant to them. If you are a tumbler struggling with a mental block (you'll learn to not call it that anymore) then you'll likely skip straight to that section, which is fine. Just make sure to go back and read everything up to that point to get the mental skills that will help you reach the level of mastery.

I also strongly believe in reading a chapter and thinking about how you can integrate it into your life and then continuing on to the next chapter. I think reading a book like this is actually an interactive experience instead of a one-way knowledge dump. I have written what I know that works from personal experience, reading research, and listening to countless people in the industry that have put thought and effort into improving. Once you read that information you will need to work with it to integrate it into your own life. Discuss it with your friends, family, coaches, or your cat if she'll listen, because talking about it, or teaching it, helps clarify and solidify these concepts in your mind.

Now, let's start your quest toward mental mastery!

A Few Motivating Quotes to Kick Things Off

'Happiness is the joy you feel while striving toward your potential'
- Shawn Achor

'The stories we tell ourselves are how we see the world'
– Dr. Joe Dispenza

'The best way to predict the future is to create it'
- Peter Drucker

'Practice makes Progress'
- unknown author

Chapter 1

Self-Esteem

Self-Esteem You can think of building self-esteem like painting a picture. You are the artist, the canvas is your self-esteem, the paints are the thoughts we have and the thoughts others have about us, and the paintbrushes (how we use the paints) are our daily actions and reactions to other people's thoughts.

As the artist, you are the one in control of how you use the paints and brushes to create your picture. And just like art, you can always change your mind partway through and do things differently. If you are already in the habit of negative self-talk or accepting others' judgments of you as the truth, rest assured your brain is capable of changing. The technical term for this is neuroplasticity. I won't bore you with a science lecture here (although it is quite fascinating, google it sometime), but I will give a brief explanation of what happens.

Your mind uses neurons to transmit messages. Your brain is constantly adjusting the neural circuits to be more efficient and to serve you better. As you repeat a skill over and over your brain wires more neurons together to make it more efficient at transmitting the stimulus. You are then able to perform the function faster and more accurately. The function can be a physical movement or a thought process. If you stop practicing a skill your brain will start to break down those connections to form new connections. So, this means, what you consistently practice you become better at. If you practice being negative, you get better at being negative. If on the other hand, you spend more time practicing being positive, then your brain will rewire circuits to become better at being positive.

Talking kindly to yourself is a good start. To see how much of a difference this can make try a little mental trick I often use when coaching. Tell yourself five things you don't like about yourself and then try a tumbling skill you can do safely. Notice how you felt while doing it and how the skill felt. Now, tell yourself five things you like about yourself, then try the same skill. Notice anything different? Chances are, after you were positive about yourself, you felt stronger, the skill felt easier, you felt better about your effort and the skill might have even made you happy! Our mindset has a huge impact on how we perform. Controlling your thoughts and keeping them positive is like a secret weapon for extra strength and greater performance. A lot of research has been done to show how big of an impact maintaining a positive mindset has on our physical well-being.

Is it always easy to do? Of course not. But with practice, it becomes easier to catch yourself when you get into those moments of negative self-talk or self-doubt. Once you are aware, you can turn your thinking around to be uplifting and positive. With time and effort your new way of thinking becomes a habit.

When you've tried something, and your results were less than you expected or hoped they would be, it is easy to fall into a negative mindset. For example, let's say you are trying your back handspring for the first time by yourself. You've worked with your coach and they have told you you're ready to do it without a spot. Your palms get a little sweaty, you start to think of what could go wrong and then you go for it! When you do, your arms buckle, your head gets close to the ground and you land on your hands and knees. Did you just fail? A lot of people would say yes. But athletes that fully understand the learning process and have healthy self-esteem would argue otherwise.

Maybe your back handspring wasn't very good from a technical standpoint, but let's look at what you just accomplished. You just pushed past a fear and tried it anyway. You now know you are courageous! You just made a huge step of progress toward your goal. You kept yourself safe by going hard to get over once you started. Now you know if you fully commit to the skill, you can at least keep yourself safe. Viewing your attempt through the correct lens allows you to see, what some might consider a failure (not doing a perfect back handspring) is in fact major progress. Doing this can boost your self-esteem, help you gain confidence, and help you get skills faster. Instead of putting yourself down for mistakes try thinking about your effort and congratulate yourself for trying hard! Then, make a plan for what you can do better with the next attempt. Realizing that mistakes are a normal part of the learning process is extremely important. It's so important I'm going to say it again, in all caps this time, REALIZING THAT MISTAKES ARE A NORMAL PART OF THE LEARNING PROCESS IS EXTREMELY IMPORTANT. When we view mistakes as opportunities to learn we get into the growth mindset and tend to stay more positive when faced with adversity or perceived failure.

Now the difficult part, when someone else puts down your attempt. At first, it is easy to take what they say as 'the truth' and an absolute. However, if we remember that other peoples' thoughts are their opinions and only their opinions, then it's easier for us to keep a positive mindset. When we have a healthy view of feedback from others, we view their opinion as something to consider. Then we get to decide if we should or need to implement it. If someone puts you down for what you just did, try one of these techniques:

1. Internally tell yourself 5 things you like about yourself
2. Think of 2 or more things you felt went well on what you just tried
3. Try sifting through their put down for something constructive you can take from their remark and focus on the positive that can come from that

Maintaining your autonomy in this way feeds into developing healthy self-esteem. Now you've taken someone else's opinion and instead of reacting to it or feeling bad, you've used your own thoughts and mind to determine how and if it should affect your life. Doing this is very empowering and helps you to realize you are in control of your life and where it goes. Life is always a series of choices; make your own choices and you will be much happier in life.

On this note, you may have heard there are two types of self-esteem. Healthy versus unhealthy. Healthy self-esteem isn't about what you eat or how much you work out. Healthy self-esteem is a positive mindset derived from within yourself. You don't rely on other people to make you feel good about yourself. When you are in a healthy self-esteem mindset, your effort is more important than your result. For example, after an attempt at a skill that didn't go as well as you'd hoped, you might ask yourself, 'did I TRY my best or my hardest?' If the answer is yes, then viewed through the lens of healthy self-esteem, you feel good about yourself and view yourself in a positive way despite not performing at your best. If the answer is 'no, I didn't try my hardest or give it my best' viewing it through healthy self-esteem means you'd see it as an opportunity to grow and try harder the next time. You might even ask yourself, 'what can I do differently next time to try harder?'

Even world-class athletes make mistakes, don't always win, don't give it their best effort at times, and fail to reach their goals. Some athletes at this level are very happy, healthy people because they view their effort as more important than the outcome. They've become comfortable with the process of learning, including being comfortable with making mistakes. Others at this level seem to walk around in a constant state of frustration and unhappiness, unfulfilled by their accomplishments. Which would you rather be? Happy about what you've done or miserable despite what you've done?

The best part is, it's a choice. That's right, you get to decide how you view the world and what makes you happy. We each have our own personality and our personalities are malleable, like putty. We can change them through the way we interact with them. There is a well-known idea about being the observer of our emotions and thoughts. Instead of letting our emotions and thoughts control our lives through reactions, we observe our emotions and thoughts and then decide how we act in response to them. When we adopt this point of view, we can see that our thoughts are happening, and we can watch them without immediately responding to them. Then we have time to decide how we want to handle them. Do we want to act on them? Or maybe we decide they aren't helpful and we let them float on by like a cloud in the sky without taking any action. This might surprise you but, you've certainly already done this many times in life.

Think about the time your sibling was extra annoying, and you had the thought of wanting to shove them but then decided (thankfully) that it was a bad idea and didn't do it. Or maybe you saw someone drop a $20 bill, and you had the thought to keep it instead of returning it to them, but you did the right thing and returned it to them. The same principles apply to all of our thoughts. We can decide if a thought fits

17

with who we want to be or not. If it does, then we decide how we act upon that thought.

Feeling good about yourself and liking who you are is the foundation of self-esteem. That foundation is built by positive self-talk, accepting that it is good to make mistakes, maintaining a growth mindset, knowing that effort is more important than outcomes, and surrounding yourself with positive people.

Positive Self-talk

How you talk to yourself matters more than how others talk to you. If you are constantly down on yourself or negative, you will feel and adopt that way of living. Luckily the opposite is true as well! When you compliment yourself, talk positively to yourself, and build yourself up you adopt that way of living and you are more likely to accomplish your goals because you view things in a positive way. When we are in a positive mindset we tap into our internal power, both emotionally and physically. Our thoughts come from a place that says 'I can do this' or 'I can figure this out.' Research has also shown that we are physically stronger when we think positively. You can leverage a lot of power simply by talking kindly to yourself.

It's interesting when you realize how closely related positive self-talk is to a growth mindset. You've heard me use the term growth mindset several times now but might still be wondering what is a growth mindset? In a phenomenal book Mindset by Carol Dweck, she describes the two types of mindsets people adopt. A fixed mindset or a growth mindset.

In a growth mindset, you have the belief that you can learn and improve at anything. A knowledge that our abilities are not limited or fixed. A belief that if we put our mind and effort into something, then we can change and improve.

Research has shown that a person's IQ, something once believed to be unchangeable, is in reality very malleable and can improve with focused learning and practice. When you have a growth mindset you see mistakes as something to learn from and embrace. Think of how much you learn when you fail at something. You learn what didn't work and if you analyze a little deeper, you learn why it didn't work. The 'why' is an important key to learning and improving. You might have heard about Thomas Edison working on his invention of the lightbulb. He tried thousands of times before he made one that worked. When a reporter asked, "How did it feel to fail 1,000 times?" Edison replied, "I didn't fail 1,000 times. The light bulb was an invention with 1,000 steps." This is a brilliant way of thinking! We don't get tumbling skills in one attempt. We get them through repeated small steps. Learning something with every step will lead you in a forward direction. Focusing on your effort and adopting a growth mindset will open up a world of possibilities to you.

Choose Your Crew Wisely

Self-esteem can also be enhanced or damaged by our social circle so be careful who you hang out with. Do your friends encourage you to be your best? Are they nice to other people? It is often said that we are the average of the five people we hang out with the most. While we cannot always control who we are around daily (our family, co-workers, etc.), we can control our responses to them. Another thing we can control is, who we choose as friends. If you are consistently nice, kind, and respectful, it is more likely those types of people will come into your life. Our behaviors reflect what comes back to us.

You might have people around you that are permanently stuck in a negative mindset and don't respond well to your positivity. It is perfectly ok to limit your contact with those people. Try by setting realistic and respectful boundaries with those people. Be direct but maintain an air of kindness and respect when setting boundaries. The trick is to be firm and clear in the boundary you're setting. Here is an example to help clarify what I mean.

Example: Someone that is generally negative invites you to go to a party. Your response might be, 'that party sounds like it would be a lot of fun, but I am not going to go. I bet you'll meet some great people there'.

Notice how you clearly state you are not going to the party, which is setting a boundary. You remain very kind and positive by letting them know they will have a fun time and meet great people there. Sandwiching the boundary, or 'no,' between compliments or kindness like I did in the example above, is a great way to set limits. You have your needs met and don't have to give in to something you don't want to do. Now take a moment to see if you can come up with some examples of your own.

Choosing happy and uplifting friends will open up a whole new set of options for you. People that are genuinely happy and positive are easy to be around. You gain comfort when around them. Their positivity increases a sense of trust. Think about it, who would you trust more, someone who is always talking negatively about people or someone who always has nice things to say about people? When you're not around that person, are you worried about what the positive person is saying about you? What about the negative person? Now might be an interesting time for you to think about how just reading those sentences makes you feel. Even though you weren't actually in that situation, chances are you felt a bit of happiness thinking about someone saying something nice about you. Compare that to the feeling of someone saying mean things about you. You probably feel mad, unhappy, or uneasy. The people we surround ourselves with is hugely important! Find the people that make you feel good about yourself. It's much easier to stay positive and develop healthy self-esteem when it surrounds you.

It has been shown that social connections can have more to do with our overall health than our genetics. Wow, that is truly powerful when you stop and think about it. Without getting too technical, here are the basics of what happens.

Your behavior, emotions, the food you eat, and stress levels all play a part in gene expression. Gene expression is responsible for creating proteins and enzymes that play an integral part in everything that happens in your body. That means that you can change your body and health simply by surrounding yourself with positive people, being grateful for what you have, eating healthy, building other people up, and maintaining a positive world view. You can create health through happiness!

Catch a Good Mood

Have you ever noticed how moods are contagious? If you are around really happy, high energy people, your mood starts to reflect this. If you are around people who are in a bad mood and low energy, after a while, your mood will start to shift to mirror theirs. A third possibility is your mood not conforming to the other person. It's then likely you will drive each other nuts. If you want to be happy, positive, and upbeat it is much easier if you surround yourself with like-minded people and friends.

You might have also noticed that people you compliment tend to compliment you back. I always feel the best compliments are sincere and genuine, something you truly feel about the person. Try expressing your positive thoughts about someone and notice how it helps brighten their day. I think one of the coolest things about it is, it also ends up putting you in a better mood. What a great way to become happy! It's a win, win for both of you.

There is a scientific reason behind this phenomenon, known as mirror neurons. To keep it light, I'll be brief in explaining. Mirror neurons are located in your brain and are responsible for the feelings you get when you just watch someone feeling an emotion. Think of when you watch someone in a movie, and you start to feel what they are feeling on the screen; those are your mirror neurons at work. They help with keeping your social connection going, especially with empathy.

What is empathy, you ask? It is the skill of putting yourself in someone else's shoes to understand what life is like for them. Empathy lacks judgment and comes from a place of understanding and connection. When you truly feel empathy for someone or something, you have a kindness about your interaction with them.

You might be wondering what does all of this have to do with tumbling? Remember how our mindset, reducing stress, and maintaining positivity leads to better performance. The more you practice these skills, the more it translates into every aspect of your life. Practicing the skills in different situations builds the foundation of mental strength it takes to excel at tumbling. Take some time right now to start applying the principles from this chapter into your life. Find some specific examples in your life where you can apply what you learned and start practicing!

Chapter 2

Self Confidence

Have you had those days where you feel extra confident and happy? It's funny how the two go hand in hand, right? What does it feel like when you feel confident?

You feel stronger, more capable, as if you could take on the world. You tap into a strong belief that you can do something and will keep trying at it with a level of determination that almost borders on compulsiveness. You feel an overwhelming sense of 'I got this!' or 'I'm going to get this!'

What made you feel that way? Wouldn't it be awesome to feel that way more often?

When you develop self-confidence, you will make huge strides in your tumbling and all aspects of life.

What does it take to build self-confidence?

1. Build on small successes over and over again.
2. Bring a level of excitement to your practice.

3. Be specific in encouraging yourself.
4. Remind yourself of your progress.
5. Compliment your efforts.
6. Find challenges exciting and engaging.
7. Reaffirm your positive behaviors when you notice them.
8. Remember that what a person believes they are, they become. Believe in your abilities.
9. Believe in your willingness to try hard and in your persistence to keep trying until you reach your goals.

Now let's go into a little more detail about some of the items in the list above.

Building on small successes puts your brain into a positive state where you gain a little bit of confidence at each step. The cool thing is, confidence builds upon itself and you start to develop a momentum of success. People often think they have to achieve huge successes to feel good about themselves, but this just isn't true. We find joy in little successes too. You experience positive feelings from anything you perceive as a win. And when we line up many of those little successes, those feelings build and build until we start to create a bigger picture of success. Before you know it, you've created a huge success too!

Breaking it Down to Make it Easier

Let me go into a little more detail here. It's easy to get overwhelmed if our goals are too big. When things feel overwhelming, we tend to shut down and not do as much or maybe not do anything at all. Our progress slows and we are more likely to give up. However, if we break the big goal into a series of smaller goals, it feels easier to make progress. We feel more empowered and less overwhelmed. Breaking them down into smaller, more easily attainable goals keeps you in a better state of mind. As we start to accomplish each of the smaller goals, we build up that momentum of success. Before long, you're significantly closer to the big goal and you can see the light at the end of the tunnel. Now you're so excited because what you once thought was impossible or improbable is within your sights, and you're almost there! That feeling of excitement adds to the momentum of success, and what started as small steps have now turned into achieving a big goal! I talk more about goal setting in the Expectations chapter later in this book.

Excitement is Powerful

Now to the next point on gaining self-confidence. Excitement! That's right when we get more excited about doing something, we gain a feeling of confidence. One of the most helpful ways to get excited is a challenge! What feels better after you've accomplished it: something that was super easy or something you really had to work for?

Hopefully, you're already on board with the natural feeling of excitement from accomplishing hard things. If not, remember what you learned before about neuroplasticity and the brain's ability to change? Read on and change the way you think.

Take a level of curious excitement into your practice and see how much it boosts your confidence. Get excited to try new things, to try to get better technique, to try a little harder than you did the last pass, get pumped up! Excitement is energy!

It's all About the Practice

Now that you're all pumped up let's talk about the difference between performance mindset and practice mindset. In my years of coaching, I've noticed that people are often stuck in the mindset that they must 'perform' every time they try a skill. We often forget that we are just practicing most of the time. Our brains are in a more playful state during practice than they are during performances. Developing skills and maintaining healthy self-esteem is easier when we are forgiving of mistakes and adopt the beginner's mindset we talked about earlier.

Our performance mindset is naturally one of trying to execute with perfection. Now, while we should be striving for greatness in our practice, the goal should not be perfection. Practice on the other hand, is all about learning. If the only thing you're learning is that you're not doing it perfectly every time, you're likely to end up in a negative mindset. However, if you're learning how to improve and you stay open to making mistakes then real progress and confidence can be built. Reminding yourself that you are just practicing will keep you in the right state of mind.

Strong Body, Strong Mind

Remember how this chapter started, with me asking you to recall those days you felt extra confident and happy and how you felt stronger on those days? Well, there is something more to this. While confidence inspires strength, strength also inspires confidence. When you feel strong you feel more capable.

It seems a lot of people have a negative view of conditioning or working out. I challenge you to change the way you think about it. Use the power of developing your physical strength to send your confidence to new heights. Take the extra steps to do conditioning and maintain good physical fitness through cross-training. Conditioning doesn't have to mean that you're doing things you hate. Find physical activities you tend to naturally enjoy. Maybe it's skiing or snowboarding you love, or hiking, running, swimming, rock climbing, etc. The list of possible activities that keep you physically fit goes on and on.

Working out can feel hard at first. Give new activities or workouts time before deciding that you don't enjoy them. Tell yourself that the activity you are doing will make you stronger and healthier. This is a great way to change your mindset. It's common that activities get more fun and enjoyable the better you get at them. Stick with it and you will start to benefit from the empowering feeling of being strong!

Chapter 3

Your Body and Mind are Connected

In an interview with Oprah, Tom Brady (considered to be the best NFL quarterback of all time) talked about how as an athlete his most important asset is his body. He takes time to ensure that he eats the best foods possible to take optimal care of his body. For him, that means avoiding fast food and eating healthy, organic whole foods. He clearly values health and vitality. As athletes, we should all consider our bodies our most important asset, even if we're not world-class. Your body is not any less valuable to you than Tom Brady's is to him. You only have one body, and only you can decide how to treat it. If you treat your body like crap, you'll feel like crap. If you treat your body well, you'll feel good.

Let's take eating as a great example. If I'm thinking about what sounds delicious then I'll likely just grab any yummy food, whether it helps my body or hurts my body. But when I think about it from the point of view of 'is this in line with my goals', I can choose things that enhance my life and make me feel better about my decisions. So instead of reaching for a donut (it does not provide the nutrition I need to be healthy or do adventurous things), I choose to take the time to get a healthier snack like a green smoothie, fruit, veggies, or even a peanut butter sandwich.

The foundation for treating your body well is to adopt values like physical health into your life. When you prioritize taking care of your body, your body, in turn, will perform better for you. Our thoughts ultimately drive the way we take care of ourselves. Some of the key aspects of providing the nutrition your body needs are:

1. Look at what the foods you eat are made of. Avoid foods with chemicals and that are highly processed. Not sure what a specific ingredient is? Then google it to see if it's something that is healthy or something you should avoid.
2. Eat enough. If you starve your body of nutrients, it will not be able to perform as well. When you are in a state of perceived famine from not eating enough, your body goes into a state of survival and cannot perform higher-level activities. It's more concerned about conserving and surviving than it is about performing.
3. Eat right. This ends up having the same outcome as not eating enough. If you eat the wrong foods (foods that are devoid of the nutrients your body needs) then your body goes into the same state of survival it does when you're not eating enough. Try choosing to eat healthy for a month and notice the differences you feel. If you've had a poor diet of processed foods and

lots of sugar it might take a little more time to adjust to the new style of eating without going back to old habits. The important thing is to try it and to be kind to yourself if you slip up. Just keep pointed at the goal and you will make it, even if you take a few steps sideways or backward. Progress is rarely if ever a straight line from where you are to where you want to be.

Did it feel like we were off on a little bit of a tangent there? Well maybe we were, but thinking about what we eat, eating right to fuel your body and mind is such an important part of the mental game it needed to be in here. We have basic physiological needs that need to be met before attempting to take on higher functioning skills like tumbling.

Visualization to Connect Your Body and Mind

It has been shown in many studies that mental practice is almost as good as physical practice. Wait… did you read that right? Yep, mental practice is almost as good as physical practice! Visualization is a powerful tool that I feel is underutilized in tumbling. Visualization can be understood as: using your mind to imagine yourself doing physical movements. There are a few key points to get the most out of visualization:

1.   When you visualize yourself doing the skill, do so from the start of the skill all the way to the end with great technique. One key is to make sure you're visualizing success on the skill every time. You want to practice

good form and being successful even when you visualize.

2. Visualize skills that are relevant to you and that you are actually working on.

3. Go through the visualization 7 to 10 times when you're lying in bed, right before you go to sleep. Then, let go of the thoughts and fall asleep. As you sleep, your brain will continue to process the information, making it even more effective.

4. Only use the visualization technique a few times per week. Like weight training, you need rest days to get stronger.

Visualization is a simple way to get extra practice and improve. When done correctly, the effects are pretty amazing. It might be hard to believe that mentally practicing something makes us more physically capable, but the research is solid. And even better than research is your own experience. Try it for a month and see if you notice a difference. I'm very confident you will.

Chapter 4

Determine What is Important to You

There are countless ways we can spend our time. It's easy to get sort of lost in menial tasks and skip over the things that are most important to us. Being able to focus on what brings us closer to our goals is an important mental skill. If you're having a hard time determining what is most important to you, try considering the following:

Think about what brings you the most joy or gives you the most sense of satisfaction.

Think about what your ideal life would be like in a year, two years, five years. Now work backward from those ideals and create some stepwise goals to see what you can do now to start working toward your dream life.

Once you figure out what is important to you and what you want your life to look like your decisions in life will be easier. Let's say you are having a hard time deciding whether or not you should try out for cheer. Maybe you've determined that connection with people and taking on challenges are important to you. You can see how joining a cheer team would satisfy both needs. You get to participate in a team sport that is based on connection to the team and you get the physical and mental challenge that is associated with becoming a cheer athlete. Trying out for the cheer team seems like an obvious choice and something worth your time and effort.

Now that you've determined it's important to you, it will help shape the decisions you make daily. Knowing it will require physical challenges you start to make better decisions on the food you eat, the exercise you do (doing exercise when you've got a reason makes it a lot more enjoyable than when you don't have a reason), the amount of sleep you get and how you spend your time in general. You'll also be more inclined to socialize with other students who will try out as well. Now you've started to create things that satisfy your desire for connection too.

Without knowing what is important to you, it could be easy to get overwhelmed by the physical aspect. You might also have a hard time attempting to connect to other aspiring cheerleaders. But once you've decisively made up your mind about what is important to you, you'll find there is little that can stand in your way of reaching your goals and living your dreams. Is it always easy? Of course not. But that's not the point. Determining what you want in life helps get you through the tougher times. We all have tough times, especially when we have big goals. It's amazing how much it helps to have a plan of smaller goals and to decide ahead of time that it is important to you. Learning to persevere through those times will take you much further in life. Deciding what is important to you is a skill. Remember, any skill takes time and practice to develop, so be kind to yourself along the way. Take a few moments to think about what is important to you and how you can use that knowledge to make decisions about how you spend your time.

Chapter 5

Managing Emotions

Emotions are powerful. They can make you do things you later regret or keep you from doing things you truly want to do. With great power comes great potential. Learning to work with your emotions and control them leads to a happier, healthier life.

Some people seem to view emotions as a problem or something to rid themselves of. The problem is, we cannot truly rid ourselves of something we are made of. Emotions are a physiological response to a stimulus. There are actual molecules coursing through your body that are responsible for emotions. While our bodies produce these emotions, we get to decide how we react to them. One cool thing is, if we apply the same principles we learned about deciding how we integrate other peoples' opinions we can gain control over our emotions as well. Some of the same concepts apply which means we get to practice those skills twice as often so we can master the skills twice as fast!

I guess the one catch here is that dealing with comments from other people can be more complicated than just dealing with your own emotions. Mainly because we also have an emotional response to other people's comments. As much as we can try to look at other peoples' comments through a logical perspective, our emotions tend to creep in and run the show. Our emotions feel even more real to us, and rightfully so. They are an interpretation of our experience. They are a reaction to what we are going through.

The beauty of it is, we have control over how we react to our emotions. We may not be able to control the feeling of frustration that comes up when we fall on a skill, but we absolutely can control how we react to that feeling of frustration. Do we get angry, stomp our feet, and throw a tantrum? Or do we pick ourselves up, decide that we will try harder next time, focus on our technique, and most importantly, congratulate ourselves on our effort? Which set of actions do you think will lead to positive results? It's kind of funny how sometimes clearly spelling things out can make the choice so obvious. It's also amazing how not stopping to think about your actions can keep someone in a negative loop of trial and frustration.

Once you realize you control your responses to your emotions, you unlock a world of hidden potential. You become the driver of what happens in your life instead of the passenger along for the unnerving ride.

Primary Versus Secondary Emotions

Sometimes the emotions are simple and easy to understand. I fell and almost got hurt; my emotion was fear. Other times the emotions aren't quite as easy to understand, or the emotion that comes up might be a secondary emotion.

You might be wondering what I mean by a secondary emotion. A secondary emotion looks and acts like the emotion causing the reactionary behavior, but it's more like a Halloween mask. A great example is anger. Anger is often a secondary emotion. It looks and feels like your mom is angry because you didn't study for your test. But if you look closer at the root cause of her anger, it's because she's worried (and possibly disappointed) that you won't pass your class and may not develop into the successful adult she knows you can be. In this case, her fear and disappointment are the primary emotions she feels, but they come out as a secondary emotion of anger. Have you seen people at the gym that get angry when they don't get a skill or fall on a pass? Their primary emotion is likely embarrassment, fear, or disappointment, but they express it through the secondary emotion of anger.

The problem with secondary emotions like anger is they are not constructive. Most of the time, if the person addresses the primary emotions, then the reaction to the situation is better and more constructive. Imagine if instead of your mom getting angry and yelling at you, she talked calmly to you about how she felt regarding her concerns, why she feels it's important to do well on tests, and reassured you that she loves you and cares about your happiness. Which situation feels like it would be more helpful, positive, and uplifting? To be clear, I'm not saying either way is going to actually change your behavior. Change is ultimately up to you. Hopefully, you can see that addressing the underlying emotions gives you a healthier view of what is really going on, so you have more information to base your decisions on.

Where does all this lead? If you try to work on being less angry without identifying the underlying emotion, you'll be trying to fix the symptom, not the problem. It would be like trying to stop a runny nose by shoving Kleenex up your nose instead of addressing the underlying cold that makes your nose run. You might get some relief with the Kleenex, but the symptoms won't truly go away until you've solved the cause. Ok, enough analogies, for now, let's get back to the practical side of how this directly applies to you and your tumbling.

Now that we know that the emotion that initially comes up might be a secondary emotion or it might be a primary emotion, we can decide how we deal with the emotion that is the root cause.

Getting Control of Your Emotions

To me, the first step to handling emotions is to be ok feeling an emotion. Then the most important aspect is to consciously decide how to act after feeling that emotion.

An important side note about fear: *Everyone feels fear. It is absolutely, without a doubt, normal and ok to feel fear. Some*

people choose to let fear stop them from doing what they want. Others seem to use it as fuel; it gives them ambition. Most fall somewhere in between. They feel fear but can usually press through and do something in a given amount of time or when their desire gets high enough.

Our goal is to become friends with fear. We acknowledge that it is there, realize that it is healthy, and know how to put it in its rightful place (to the side). We can then accomplish our goals and create the life we want. One interesting thing about fear is it is actually a useful emotion. When we feel fear, our senses become heightened, so we are more aware and in tune with what we are doing. It brings about a level of focus that can be very helpful when we get comfortable with it and use it properly.

When we become ok with an emotion, the resistance to that emotion goes away, and we can more easily deal with it. Somehow being ok with an emotion takes away some of its power, so we can then decide more easily how to handle our response to that emotion. If we're too focused on trying not to feel fear, then we're using our brain's capacity and effort to resist it rather than using our thoughts to figure out how to move it out of the way to perform the skill we are attempting.

In his exceptional book, 'Your Brain at Work,' author David Rock discusses methods for dealing with emotions and handling situations in more productive manners. He discusses the need to label simple emotions and to reappraise more complex emotions.

Let's start with what David Rock refers to as labeling. Simple, less complex emotions can often be handled by simply labeling them. By consciously putting a label on the emotion, we gain some power and control over the situation. It involves being aware of what you are going through or being in a state of mindfulness. When we are aware, we can decide to enter into the state where we can change. It is very difficult to change something we are not aware of. Labeling an emotion gives us a sort of target to direct our thoughts and actions toward. Once we label the feeling in our body as fear, we can start to use methods to lessen the fear. Those methods will be different than how we handle the feeling in our body we label as embarrassment.

More powerful or more complex emotions require more powerful methods of dealing with them. Reevaluating a situation through a different perspective is what David Rock considers reappraising. Sometimes we get hit with emotions or situations that are so hard or complicated that simply labeling them is not powerful enough to change our response to them. The emotions still seem to roll right over our thoughts and produce reactions instead of thoughtful action. However, sometimes all we need is a little shift in perspective about the situation to realize that we are still in control. In tumbling, if you fall on a skill instead of focusing on how you almost got hurt, try looking at it from a slightly different perspective. Ask yourself, what can I learn from how I fell? Or maybe you point out to yourself, 'look how well

I fell.' When you can change a negative, 'I almost got hurt' to a positive, 'look how well I fell and rolled out of it,' the same situation takes on a whole new feeling and outcome. Now the next time you try the skill, instead of being scared that you might fall and get hurt, you'll be more confident. You know that you will keep yourself safe and avoid injury because you fell correctly the previous time.

Self-fulfilling Prophecies

I think the most powerful tool for managing emotions and creating the life you want is related to the quote at the beginning of the book from Dr. Joe Dispenza, "The stories we tell ourselves are how we see the world." The tool I'm talking about is the powerful tool/weapon of self-fulfilling prophecies. When a person decides on an outcome before they are in a situation and they subconsciously do things to ensure that outcome, that is a self-fulfilling prophecy. Generally, when people talk about self-fulfilling prophecies they are talking about the negative side to it. The way people will unconsciously self-sabotage to make a negative outcome happen just to reinforce their thoughts or fears. It's amazing how our brain likes to do things to prove it is right, even if it's actually harmful to us.

However, in the right hands, self-fulfilling prophecies can yield great results as well. Let's take a look at what a self-fulfilling prophecy is made of.

1. There is a person that does the thinking, the deciding, and ultimately carries out the plan.
2. There are actions that will be taken along the way.

3. There is the outcome, the result of the actions.
4. There is a time designated for when the outcome will happen.
5. And finally, there is the pre-described plan of reaction to the outcome.

What's interesting is, a lot of what happens is driven by our subconscious thoughts. Things we don't even realize are happening unless we pay particular attention to our actions and thoughts.

Since we are interested in learning a skill that will help improve your tumbling let's take a look at an example of how you can create a positive self-fulfilling prophecy regarding tumbling.

A person, let's say you, decides they really want to get their standing tuck. You've heard from other people that they are scary and hard. Now you have a choice. Will you ignore what they are saying and just take your own experience as it comes? Or are you going to just adopt their point of view before you've even tried?

If you just adopt what they say, you will likely do things subconsciously to reinforce that decision. This includes dismissing your feelings about it, even if it feels easy for you. You might even consciously think something to the effect of, 'this is supposed to be hard, there's no way I just almost did that,' and you will unintentionally limit your potential. You might subconsciously do things to reinforce your thoughts of how hard or scary it is.

Alternatively, let's say you decide to hear what they have to say but decide that you will try it and that you will get it in several months. After all, everyone is different and has their strengths. You decide from the beginning that you will get your standing tuck no matter the time or work involved. You are now free to create your own thoughts and actions surrounding the skill. You start to practice the form, thinking about every important aspect. You notice they don't seem that hard after all! You decide to try your best and maintain a positive outlook. It starts to feel easier the more you focus on proper form. You set realistic expectations. You know it can be easy at times, but sometimes it can feel hard or scary. You have learned how to effectively deal with these emotions. Going into it, you have a plan of action. You've decided in advance that your positive actions keep you progressing. Before you know it, you're getting closer and closer to doing your standing tuck by yourself. Each small success builds on the prior small success, until you've built a lot of positive momentum. Then one day, you get it! Just like you decided you were going to do at the beginning. Congratulations, you've just completed a positive self-fulfilling prophecy. By implementing some mental skills, you got your standing tuck!

This is a powerful tool. Accomplishing a goal that seems lofty or hard creates a deep feeling that you have the power to reach whatever you set your mind to. Feeling empowered is one of the greatest gifts you can give yourself. Getting to that point is like anything else in life, it requires consistent effort, the correct mindset, and making small steps that lead to big results. Once you get to a point where you feel empowered it is easier to maintain.

Try to recognize when you're getting into a positive feedback loop where the actions you take and the thoughts you have build you up. When you realize you are in one, keep it going! Imagine it like a fire within you. Keep stoking it to make it burn brighter. Remember, our thoughts become our reality and our reality helps fuel our thoughts.

Chapter 6

Focus and Flow

Athletes often talk about getting into a state of flow when they are performing well. The state of flow can be understood as: a time when your mental focus and physical execution are synched so well that your performance feels almost effortless. You enter a type of zone where the rest of the world disappears and all you are focused on is what you are doing. When we can get into this state of flow on a regular basis our progress takes off. So how do we willingly and consistently get into this magical state of flow?

Here are a few tips and tricks to try. Each person will find their own path into their flow, but these ideas can get you started.

1. Use a soft focus with your eyes.
2. Relax your face in a soft but concentrated gaze with a slight smile.
3. Get into a rhythm with your movements. Use music to help get you into the rhythm.

4. Slow, steady belly breathing, in for four seconds and out for four seconds.
5. Be aware of your feet on the floor so you can ground yourself.
6. As you go for your skills, focus on your form, and let your mind be clear of distracting thoughts. Use mantras to help (see Chapter 9 for more information about Mantras).

Remember how we talked about mindfulness near the beginning of the book? Practicing mindfulness makes it easier to slip into a state of flow. The two are related. If you have a hard time being present in a moment it can be harder to get into a state of flow. There are a lot of great guided meditations online that can help you develop mindfulness and presence. I highly recommend finding a few to try out. Not all are created equal so try several from different people to find the style you like best. Once you've started to notice what the feeling of being 100% present feels like, see if you can notice a similar feeling when you get into a state of flow, either when tumbling or another activity like running or swimming.

Chapter 7

Expectations

Life is full of expectations. Some we put on ourselves, others we adopt from what other people expect from us. Either way, the expectations that affect how you behave are ultimately up to you. Let's look at an extreme example to get the point. If someone expects you to steal something, it is up to you to decide if that expectation will alter your behavior. If your value system is strong, then you will not be swayed by their expectations. If you're unsure how you feel about stealing, you may let someone else's idea determine what you do. The point is, you get to decide what you do with the expectations others try to put on you. The best way to know what to do with others' expectations is to really get to know yourself and what is important to you personally.

One of the most important things to understand about expectations is that they can be a major source of stress. If you've set unrealistic expectations for yourself, then your stress level will be dramatically elevated. One reason this is particularly damaging is that stress inhibits performance. Stress impairs our mental and physical abilities. So now, not only have you set expectations that aren't realistic, but you've also lowered your ability to perform at your best. How likely do you think it is that you will reach your expectations at this point? Not very likely, right?

Setting and holding yourself to unrealistic expectations can be very demotivating. Decisions become very overwhelming, often preventing you from even knowing when or where to start. Instead of gaining confidence through accomplishing goals and reaching expectations, you end up feeling bad about not progressing or accomplishing what you set out to do.

On the other hand, if you set reasonable expectations it can help motivate you to push harder or to follow through. You're probably wondering, how do I set realistic expectations? Although it is not an exact science, there are a couple things you can keep in mind when dealing with expectations.

1. First, and most important, is to go into the situation with a mindset that expectations can and will change. Setting and resetting expectations is a great skill to develop. You may go into a situation with unrealistically high expectations but not know any better until you are knee-deep in the process

2. Constantly evaluating and revaluating where you are at in relation to your expectations is a healthy and helpful thing to do. Resetting expectations is a skill

that requires practice. You will benefit the most if you maintain a growth mindset. Just a quick reminder, a growth mindset is where you look at mistakes as learning opportunities and that you always have the ability to learn and grow.

Goal Setting

Goal setting is inherently related to expectations. There are so many books written about goal setting so I'll just take you through the most important aspects of how to create helpful, realistic goals. The bottom line for how to make goal-setting work for you is actually a very simple recipe:

1. Set a timeline for the goal with a definitive end date that is within a month or two of setting the goal.
2. Make the goal specific about something measurable. For example: Instead of saying 'I want to do a good back handspring' try setting the goal to be 'I want to do my back handspring with straight legs ten times in a row'.
3. Make it something that challenges you but is reasonable for you to attain with hard work and determination in the time frame given.
4. Try as hard as you can to reach the goal. If you don't reach your goal at the end of the time allotted, then reframe the goal into a new goal. This way, you're not dwelling on not reaching a goal. Instead, you see it as an opportunity to keep growing and learning.

There is a sort of art form to goal setting and completion. Sometimes we set goals that we accomplish very fast, so maybe we set the bar a little too low. Or sometimes we set the bar so high that it seems we'll never make it. When we set lofty goals, it can be tempting to restructure the goal midstream when it gets hard, and we seem to be a long way off. Instead of completely backing off on the goal, first try breaking the goal down into smaller, more achievable step goals that build upon each other to get you to the desired big goal.

If you're having a hard time coming up with smaller step goals try thinking of it in terms of, 'if I could do this, then I would be ready to do the next step toward the bigger goal.' Breaking a skill down into its parts is a good start. Sometimes, it can be helpful to start with the end in mind and work backward to where you need to start. Ask your coach for guidance on this if you're feeling stuck. They should have a good understanding of how to break the skill down into smaller parts.

The Power of Seed Goals

Mentally preparing for stressful or difficult situations is extremely helpful. This is very closely related to the positive use of self-fulfilling prophecies (remember that concept from the Managing Emotions chapter?). When we rehearse how we might feel, what we might encounter and how we would like to act before going into a situation then we are more likely to perform in the way we want. We also lower the stress of the situation because we feel like we've encountered it before, even though all we have done is mentally practice it. Planting seed goals does exactly this.

If you are too nervous to try a new skill, to go to the next level on a particular skill, or are having an off day, then try to plant some seed goals during your practice. Here are some examples of seed goals: 'next practice I'm going to do my round off tuck without a spot', or 'next week I'm going to add a whip in the middle of my pass'. Having a goal to mentally process in the time between practices is very helpful. Your mind gets to think about it, get nervous and work through it over and over again before you physically try it. This helps prepare your brain for how to think about it and deal with the actual situation once you are in it. The more you prepare, the better you will do.

Seed goals are shorter-term goals than our normal goals, but they follow the same principles of having a measurable outcome and a defined time frame. While seed goals are most helpful when it is something you are nervous about, you can always use seed goals to mentally prepare for the progress you want to make in your next practice as well. Remember, with seed goals; you are just planting the idea of something you want to do. Your conscious and subconscious minds go to work to help make it a reality.

Chapter 8

Progression

When you understand what a typical progression in a sport like tumbling looks like it can help you stick through the rough spots to get back to the times of major growth and progress. Since so much of tumbling is building upon the skills you've previously learned, it is imperative that you focus on the correct form from the beginning to keep your progress as consistent as possible. Plateaus are normal in tumbling but focusing on form and thoughtful practice will minimize the time you spend in the plateau phase. A typical learning curve for tumbling is to make a lot of relatively fast progress in the beginning, hit a little bit of a plateau, make another upward spike in progress followed by another plateau, and repeat. See figure 8.1

To thoroughly understand what we go through when learning new skills let's take a minute to look at it from a higher level and then we'll drill down into more details.

The basic steps we take when learning a skill:

1. We must have an understanding of what we are trying to learn.
2. We start practicing the movements. Sometimes isolated parts of the whole movement and sometimes the entire skill as one.
3. We keep practicing and refining our ability to do the movements/skill.
4. We get to the point where we can repeatedly do the skill without assistance and without much conscious thought about the parts.

Now let's dig in a little deeper and get to the more interesting details of what is going on. Once we understand the details, we can go back for another high-level look at what typical progressions look like in physically and mentally challenging sports like tumbling.

1. We must understand what we are trying to learn. Being able to visually see or cognitively understand what the skill should look like is imperative to learning. Gaining a thorough understanding of the technique involved in a skill makes learning the skill easier. When your brain already completely understands what your body is trying to do, you can make adjustments and improvements faster. Spend time when you're introduced to a new skill to thoroughly understand the technique, and you'll notice a profound difference in your progression.

2. Practicing the movements. Then we move into physically repeating the movements and helping our body to feel what is expected of it. Our body starts learning the complex and subtle movements and starts to develop neurological shortcuts to make us more efficient at the movements. Our muscle memory starts developing, and we can perform more of the skill without directly thinking about it. Focusing on proper form and movement from the beginning will develop the proper muscle memory that will help your progression in tumbling stay more consistent.

Drills are particularly helpful for developing the proper form and muscle memory for each part of a skill. The more you can break a skill down into its parts and learn each part really well the better you will perform the entire skill. While we cannot always do tumbling skills slow, we can do parts slowly through drills.

Some research suggests that we learn faster and more completely when we slow down what we are learning. In an interview with Jim Kwik author Tim Larkin talks about; when people training in the military have something that is extremely important or dangerous to learn they slow learning down to 40% or slower speed. Having a coach spot you through a skill or drill to aid in slowing it down can have major benefits to your long-term learning and progress. Even visualizing the skill slowly will help.

3. Keep practicing and refining. Now we're really starting to gain some momentum with making progress toward getting the skill by ourselves. We need to continue to focus on using good form; otherwise, our muscle memory will start to shift away from good form. It is important to remember that our bodies and minds are continually changing, which means that bad form can take over or good form can take over. What we practice is what we perform. Relearning skills because we have to retrain our muscle memory is one of the most frustrating experiences for tumblers and often leads to quitting the sport. The good news is if we focus on proper form from the beginning and throughout the third phase, our progress through the skill and onto the upper skills will be a lot smoother and more enjoyable. In the third phase, we start to feel our technique in our body even more.

4. We can do the skill repeatedly without assistance. Now, many people think that once they can do a skill once without assistance, they 'have' the skill. The danger of thinking this way is it sets you up for unrealistic expectations. With tumbling, doing a skill once without assistance is an important step toward 'having' a skill. To truly have a skill you should be able to safely and repeatedly perform the skill with reasonably good technique. During the fourth phase, we do not get to relax about the technique. Our muscle memory is solidly formed at this point, but remember that our bodies and mind can be rewired.

The good news is that since you've practiced the proper technique so many times it takes a lot less effort to maintain it than it does to build it. It also takes a lot more to lose the muscle memory than it would have in the earlier phases. The catch here is that if you get to this phase with bad technique the rewiring concept still holds true. Meaning, it takes a lot more time and effort to retrain the bad technique to become good technique and to develop the new muscle memory. Combine the physical rewiring with the (harder) mental component and 'fixing' a skill can be extremely frustrating for a tumbler and may even lead to quitting the sport they've dedicated so much time and effort to.

As mentioned above, progress in tumbling is not a straight line learning curve. It is more like steps, where bursts of progress are followed by shorter plateaus. Our goal as tumblers is to make the plateaus as short as possible. The plateaus are hard to deal with mentally. If a plateau turns into a backslide it becomes even more difficult to work through. Understanding that with consistent effort, practice, a few mental tricks you've learned in this book, and a positive attitude, you can work through any plateau or backslide. While good coaching will help keep you off the plateaus for as long, it is not solely up to your coach to keep you progressing. It is your hard work and determination that makes all the difference in your progress.

Figure 8.1: A normal progression in tumbling

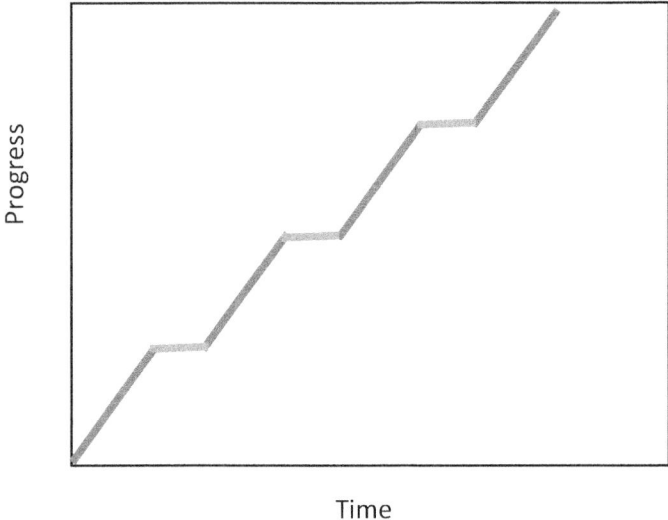

Time

Fig. 8.1 *The diagonal lines (blue) represent the time you are making progress on a skill. The horizontal lines (orange) represent the plateaus where progress slows. You and your coach work together to get you off the plateaus as fast as possible.*

The Importance of Muscle Memory in Progression

Developing muscle memory for proper form will keep you progressing and help keep you from plateauing. Every time you perform a skill you are either enhancing or relying on muscle memory to help perform that skill. Take your time to think about each turn and what the proper form of the skill is. Then try your best to implement it every time. Now, it is pretty clear that not every time you do a skill it is going to have exceptional form. However, if your form was a little off you can still follow through with form even if it's after the skill is done to develop the muscle memory.

For example, you may be trying to get a good rebound out of a back handspring where you land with your feet slightly in front and arms up so you can add a second back handspring. If you land with your feet behind you and your arms down you can still develop the muscle memory by quickly bringing yourself into the position you are trying to hit, arms up and feet in front. Another great example is practicing back walkovers or backbend kickovers. Instead of just coming up with your arms down, get in the habit of pushing off with your hands and bringing your arms up to finish. Practice following through on form to develop muscle memory more quickly.

Developing your muscle memory on the smaller, but often overlooked, parts of skills makes a huge difference in maintaining your upward progression. Shaping drills are also specifically designed for isolating parts of skills to develop muscle memory. Thoughtful practice always leads to better and faster results than just trying something over and over again as fast as you can. Be patient and thoughtful, and your tumbling skills come together faster and with less stress.

There is one final key to making progress:

Challenges. One of the best things you can do mentally to elevate your progression is to fall in love with challenges. Think about it. If you're not being challenged are you going to progress? Maybe, but probably very slowly. Find the joy in being challenged. If something feels too easy, then ask your coach for a challenge! Turn your tumbling practice into sort of a game where you take on challenges and conquer them. Tumbling should be fun!

Chapter 9

Mental Blocks

What are mental blocks? How do they develop? And most importantly, how do you get over one? While coaching in the gym, I don't use the term 'mental block,' and I'll explain why in a little bit. However, for ease and clarity in this book, I will use the term liberally.

As you learn tumbling a few things are happening in your body and mind. You are developing neural pathways for the specific movements of the skills. The more you practice the skill the more efficient you get at conveying the necessary neural signals to your body parts. This process is how we develop muscle memory. Muscle memory simply explained, is the phenomenon where once you have practiced a movement so many times your body can perform the movement 'on autopilot.' You no longer have to think about how to do it. The classic example is riding a bike. Once you learn your body always remembers how to do it without you having to think about pushing the pedals and steering the handlebars. The same thing happens in tumbling. After so much practice, your body knows how to do a back handspring without you even thinking about all the steps involved. Pretty cool, right? Well, mental blocks come in when your conscious mind gets in the way of what your body already knows how to do. Some tumblers will develop a mental block from a bad fall, from a growth spurt, from stress unrelated to tumbling, and unfortunately, some from copycat behavior. The good news is, once it has formed the methods for moving past it are the same.

Stress is the Enemy Here

Cortisol is the primary stress hormone responsible for our fight or flight response. While cortisol is healthy and normal in your daily functioning, too much of it at the wrong time puts us in a negative stress state, which inhibits our performance. Once you have a mental block increasing the stress around it will only hold you in that state longer. You might be wondering, 'how do I keep from stressing over a stressful situation?'

Remember the quote from Dr. Joe Dispeza at the beginning of the book – 'the stories we tell ourselves are how we see the world.' Well, the same is true for how we see ourselves. When we tell ourselves over and over again that we have a mental block or that we are not good at something we first start to believe it, then we start to identify with it, and then the most damaging part is we start to reinforce it. (Remember the part about negative self-fulfilling prophecies earlier in this book?)

Our minds are built to make shortcuts for the things we practice over and over again. This means when we think a thought over and over our brain gets better and faster at thinking that thought. The neurons in your brain actually start to 'wire together' to make those thoughts easier for you to have. Building those thought patterns takes time, as does replacing those thought patterns with new thought patterns. Giving yourself the space and time to reform your habitual thoughts around a given skill or set of skills is imperative for making progress. You want to approach it from a place of openness and kindness to yourself. When you expect a quick fix or perfection you set yourself up for disappointment, frustration, and stress. When you view it as a process and something to practice, you get the benefit of learning from mistakes and building confidence from the gains you've made. You also develop the important feeling of being in control of yourself.

Here are some useful, proven methods for defeating stress (the enemy) and regaining your confidence in your tumbling:

One of the most powerful things you can do to get over a mental block is to change how you think about it. Stop calling it a mental block and start identifying the emotions you feel when you won't go on a skill. Once you understand the emotions, you have something tangible to work with. Calling it a mental block gives you something negative to attach to and identify with. This label tends to put you in a fixed mindset. To get over a mental block you need to be in a growth mindset (if you skipped ahead, read the section on growth mindsets in the self-esteem chapter). I always tell my students to think of it as 'they HAD a mental block, but we're not calling it that anymore; it's in the past now'. If they continue to refer to it as a mental block, I remind them to add 'that I used to have and I am getting over.'

To start moving forward in getting your skills back, ask yourself: What are the emotions you feel when you step up to do the skill? Chances are you feel nervous, scared, embarrassed, fearful, like you're going to die, or flustered. Or maybe you're feeling all of those things at the same time.

Remember what we've learned throughout this book:

1. Labeling your emotions is a mental tactic to help deal with them. If the emotions are too powerful for labeling, then you can reappraise them by changing the way you look at the situation.
2. Stress inhibits performance and makes it harder to get into your state of flow. Labeling your feelings and reappraising the situation lowers your stress.
3. Describe to yourself what you are feeling and the physical sensations you are experiencing. Once you gain an awareness of what you're going through, then you can change it. Awareness is the basis of change.
4. Once we are aware of what is happening, we get into a state of mindfulness. Our awareness makes it easier to choose what we want to feel and where we want to put our energy.
5. Use visualization to successfully practice the skill over and over again. Remember, mental practice is almost

as good as physical practice! When it comes to getting over mental blocks, I think visualization is a powerful tool that everyone should use.

6. Set realistic expectations and goals. Use the power of seed goals.

Try Something New

Another way to make progress on regaining your skills is to approach your tumbling as an experiment. Instead of focusing on attitudes like 'this one thing will fix it, and if it doesn't, then I can't fix it' try approaching the whole situation like an experiment. Try something multiple times, try it in different ways, switch up the way you try it, take note of what you've felt, and what makes a difference for you personally. Remember, just because it did or did not work for someone else has no bearing on whether or not it will work for you. If you're feeling frustrated because you're feeling a lack of progress toward getting your skills back, remember that it will be a process, one that takes time but will be so worth it once it all comes together for you.

Bring a New Level of Determination to Your Practice

Related to treating it as an experiment, and it just might be even more important, is to decide with your whole being, all your might, that you will do things a new way. When you decide with conviction that you are going to change and do something differently, nothing can stop you. Now I'm not saying it's going to be easy, but when you make that decision your level of determination comes up to where it needs to be to press through the hard times. To keep going when progress slows or feels like it comes to a halt. When you've decided wholeheartedly that you will move into the new you, the one who used to be too nervous about doing a skill will be left behind in the past, and you'll be sailing to new heights. Setting your expectations that it will come with consistent effort and determination and that it will take time takes a lot of pressure off. And if you remember, taking the pressure off reduces the stress, which in turn enhances your performance and keeps you more positive. Then try to tap into the power of small successes to fuel your fire to keep striving to improve and overcome.

Check In With Your Breath

As you step up to try a skill or pass that you're nervous about chances are you are breathing in a somewhat stressed state. You can lower your stress and regain control by paying attention to your breath. When you focus on your breath it will bring you into a calmer, more focused state.

Notice how you are breathing. Our body and mind take signals from how we breathe. If your breaths are short and shallow, where you just breathe into your upper chest, you have a physiological response of stress. However, when you incorporate belly breathing, where your diaphragm gets involved, it puts you into a calm state and physically relaxes your body and mind. Try breathing through your nose for four seconds in and four seconds out and pulling the breath into your belly. *An interesting fact about your body; it was made to breathe through your nose. When you breathe through your nose, it warms and humidifies the air, which aids in oxygen absorption and waste removal in the lungs.* If you're ever feeling stressed out or anxious, focus on taking a couple of minutes of belly breathing through your nose and notice how it calms you down, physically and mentally.

Use Mantras

One of my favorite tools for overcoming mental blocks is to use mantras. Mantras are short, relevant sayings that you repeat to yourself as you perform something. Repeating them in your head is just fine, no need to say them out loud. When you repeat a mantra it occupies your mind enough to distract you from thinking thoughts that make you nervous or that can stop you from going on a skill. Try some out and see how powerful this tool can be!

A few examples to try:

1. In your back handspring, say 'jump hard, arms hard.'
2. For your standing tuck, say 'jump hard, arms hard, fast knees.'
3. For a twisting full, say 'set, toes up, pull.'

Come up with some mantras that isolate the important parts of the skill and are easy to remember. The key is to keep them short, so you can say them quickly and repeatedly as you go through the skill. You can even get in a rhythm while saying them and going for the skill. This can help get you into a state of flow, which also helps with performance.

A few more quick tips to help you get through a mental block or to just increase your mental game:

1. When you start to feel nervous take that as a cue to mentally focus on form and go hard.
2. Pay attention to your body position and body language – posture brings about emotions.

   It has been shown that slumping over puts you into a negative state of mind more easily. It has also been shown that standing up tall and proud puts you into a positive mindset. In a phenomenal TED Talk, 'Your Body Language May Shape Who You Are' by Amy Cuddy, she talks about the 'Power Pose'. Basically, the power pose is a winner's stance where your arms are up in the air, chin and chest are lifted, and you're smiling. Think of what people look like when they win a race.

   Doing that pose before you start a pass might make you feel uncomfortable or maybe embarrassed. But you can adopt a modification of the power pose. I call it the 'I got this' posture. In the 'I got this' posture your is chin up, eyes slightly up, shoulders back, stand proud, slight smile, and you can keep your arms down. Watch some high-level gymnasts and see how many of them will get into a pose like this before they launch down the runway to do a vault.
3. Remember to use positive self-talk to rewire your brain. When we feel positive and good about

ourselves, we are physically stronger and more capable.

4. Before you go on a skill you're nervous about, combine the 'I got this' posture with telling yourself three things you like about yourself. These are subtle things you can do in your mind and without notice but will make a huge difference.

Mental blocks are something that you can overcome. Be kind to yourself. Use the skills you learned throughout this book and keep practicing them. Expect that it will take time to get over mental blocks, but you will get there with consistent effort.

Chapter 10

Recap

Congratulations you now know a lot of mental skills that will take your tumbling to new heights! The best part is that these skills also apply to so many things. So even when you're old like your parents, you can still use these skills to enhance your life.

A quick recap of what you learned throughout this book:

You know the importance of healthy self-esteem and self-confidence. And you know how to develop both. This book taught you how important it is to surround yourself with the right people.

You learned about your brain's ability to rewire itself to change how you think. Remember about the power of adopting a growth mindset? I thought so. It's so powerful when you realize that you have the capacity to change things about yourself that were once thought to be fixed.

You now know about the power of positive thinking and its ability to make you physically stronger. The other side of that is where negativity makes you weaker and keeps you stuck.

How cool is it that you now know some skills to manage your emotions? It feels good when you realize you're in control of how you react to your emotions.

Now, think about all the cool skills you learned to get past or avoid a mental block.

And maybe the most important thing you learned in this book is that life is about learning and growing. That it's ok to make mistakes because mistakes are a normal part of moving forward. Strive for greatness and to always improve. Remember that learning is a process, not a destination. Stay curious, fall in love with challenges, reference this book often, talk to others to share the knowledge and to learn from them. Be that positive force in your gym that encourages others along their journey too. Take what you've learned here and practice, practice, practice it. 'Practice Makes Progress!'

Thank you for taking this journey with me toward mental mastery and strength!

About the Author

Jarom Perry started his career in the gymnastics world in 2006. He has coached, managed, owned and operated gyms since then. In that time, he has used the tools outlined in this book to help a multitude of students gain self-confidence through tumbling and overcome mental blocks. He has trained many coaches over the years to use the same tactics with great success.

Self-improvement is an area of psychology that Jarom is deeply fascinated by and has studied independently for decades. Jarom also has a deep seeded desire to help others live their best lives and to reach their goals and dreams. Publishing this book is one small step toward that big goal.

Printed in Great Britain
by Amazon

33507765R00046